# WORLD ENOUGH

MAUREEN N. McLANE  **WORLD ENOUGH**

FARRAR, STRAUS AND GIROUX   NEW YORK

FARRAR, STRAUS AND GIROUX

18 West 18th Street, New York 10011

Distributed in Canada by D&M Publishers, Inc.

Printed in the United States of America

First edition, 2010

Library of Congress Cataloging-in-Publication Data

McLane, Maureen N.

World enough / Maureen N. McLane.— 1st ed.

p. cm.

ISBN 978-0-374-29295-9 (alk. paper)

I. Title.

PS3613.C5687 W67 2010

811'.6—dc22

2009043085

Designed by Quemadura

www.fsgbooks.com

1 3 5 7 9 10 8 6 4 2

I see thee in thick clouds and darkness on America's shore.

WILLIAM BLAKE, *AMERICA: A PROPHECY*


—Eh! qu'aimes-tu donc, extraordinaire étranger?

—J'aime les nuages ... les nuages qui passent

... là-bas ... là-bas ... les merveilleux nuages!

CHARLES BAUDELAIRE, "L'ÉTRANGER"


The Earth is the basis of the knowledge with which we
began our specialized and detailed studies of the Moon.

HARRISON H. SCHMITT, "THE MOON BEFORE APOLLO"


... the clouds, breathing arguments ...

LISA ROBERTSON, *THE WEATHER*

# CONTENTS

## I

## II

## III

I

.

.

.

# ROUNDEL

The sea's in the dolphin, the sun's
in the rose. The stars in my lungs
are breathing. The cloud's in the rain
the sea's in.

Time to unlink every chain
linking doing to what's been done
to doing again and again—

the seas in the dolphin the suns
in the rose are the stars my lungs
breathe in the clouds in the rain
the sea's in.

# THEY WERE ALWAYS THINKING

they were always thinking
about the weather
as if they were farmers . . .

the cedars grew taller
each year till they would grow
no further—

a finished sky, a plane
gliding above the still cedars

this was the end of thinking
the trees arrested in an undying blue

the weather forever
the same as if painted

# PREMISE

the weather itself
political and not a proximate
cause of politics
or history? This
a new thing new
like atoms split
by decisive men?
Adam before
in nature
went critically
explosive full power
before an hour
or minute or unit
was humanized & ticked
atomic. Nothing
in nature that is ours
is ours. But hours
I claim abandoned
to the mood
of a day a wayward
woman wayward
life a stray word
erring all the way
down the littered street

# CHESAPEAKE BAY

Is Chesapeake Bay dead?
and the million jungled species
annihilated before the scientists
could name them?
Amazing the world
isn't enshrouded
in general mourning
unless that's what we call
the sky. I refuse
that veil. I put off
that wail. Nor will I blow
rhetorical trumpets
for morning upon morning
as if the sun weren't a stupid thing
hungry to greet us each day—
dumb yellow dog
in the sky. So faithful
that sun. Older
than any god
he never blinks
his unwondering eye.
He's watching the days
pass by our passing by.

# PASSAGE I

little moth
I do not think you'll escape
this night

I do not think
you'll escape this night
little moth


bees in clover
summer half over
friends without lovers


I bite a carrot
horsefly bites me


I thought it was you
moving through the trees

but it was the trees

I thought it was your finger
grazing my knee

it was the breeze

I thought prayers were rising
to a god alive in my mind

they rose on the wind

I thought I had all the time
and world enough to discover what I should

when it was over

I thought I would always be young
though I knew the years passed

and knowing turned my hair gray

I thought it was a welcome
what I took for a sign—

the sun . . . the unsymboling sun . . .

■

watch the clouds
on any given day
even they don't keep their shape
for more than a minute

sociable shifters
bringing weather from elsewhere
until it's our weather
and we say now it's raining here

■

Vermont shore lit
by a fugitive sun
who doesn't believe
in a day's redemption

■

sunset renovation
at the expected hour
but the actual palette
still a surprise

■

gulls alit on the lake
little white splendors
looking to shit on the dock

■

little cat
kneading my chest
milkless breasts
take your pleasure
where you can

■

not that I was alive
but that we were

# L.A.

Let me say first
    oleanders—oleanders and cactus abounded
    as if commandeered to grace a set
        idea of the place. And

        the pastel stucco'd rows
and London planes lining the sidewalked
    avenues as if anyone walked
        or biked and England
        existed. These

        are stereotypes
    so let's sing them
        in stereo:

    *I love L.A.*      *I love L.A.*

    and what is nature
    but the about-to-be-
    transformed or the never-
    to-be or whatever
    is & is & is and lacks
        a finishing touch—

The pools imply a plein air delinquency
the Hockney blue of this one
its kidney shape echoing
my two
as I've been taught by beans
and X-rays and forensic
anatomists

a gaggle of kids kibitzing
round a common table
the great American mashup visible
at the poolside bar

the children of the Pacific
the Sikh black-beturbaned
and perhaps scimitared
& other faces shining Spanish and indigene
announce a west so beautiful
and confabulated the idea
of the desert recedes

## PASSAGE II

particulars of a life
again erased

in a walk
by a river

surprisingly free
of its old pollutants

metaphor
of renewal

you too might
apply

if you knew
how to construe

in full
bloom pear

tree lacerating
the cold

air white
delicate

blossoms
a rebuke

∎

panoply
of tulips

ballet
tiger
etc

choice and abundance
delirium

of capital
cities

and suburbs
redolent

of mulched
wealth

in a mosque
tens or hundreds

dead and what
are they to me

and what is he
to hecuba
etcetera

enlist
in a nonexistent

draft
or resist

explicitly
or persist

deaf dumb mute
as ever

tra-la-la
la-la
la

■

spring bollux
my fault

my salt
my sweat

these tears
many years

what is called thinking
is obsessing

■

insectory
refectory

holy of holies
lacewings predaceous

on those creatures
who would invade

our little gardens

■

thanks for helping me
finish the bordeaux

and that peculiar
german white

before your flight
into the world

uncharted by lieder
or chansons

⬛

as if she had all the time
in the world

and that syllable
could fill it

melismatic
swirl

⬛

download
this

melancholy
bliss

iTunes
Indiana dunes

regret
you bet


al green
did not foresee me

ok al
i play you anyhow

the ex
did not foresee

what would be
nor i

his family
now in repose

inured to blues
or wrecks of soul

# SONG OF THE LAST MEETING

A few roses were blooming
on the almost bare trellis.
Your hair was now short.
I had never seen you that way.

All morning I'd wondered
whether to wear this
or that skirt.
It might have mattered.

It was strange to see you
in a new house
shining as you sat
in a necklace of raw flowers.

And when later in the café
you were so quick to flare
at any casual thing I said
I saw how you must have flashed
for all your lovers.

II

Sun through the thick glass
Another morning come—
Dreams done dawn passed
Sun through the thick glass
A faint light, the day's cast.
What's done is done and done.
Sun through the thick glass,
Another morning. Come.

■

To want to be awake
Every hour, to miss nothing
Of the changeable air, the lake.
To want to be awake
In the light and starred dark—
Every instant another thing
To want. To be awake
Every hour. To miss nothing.

■

A tender mist barely there
In the morning. A soft sun,
Dew on the grass, light chill in the air—

A tender mist barely there.
August near over. What to make clear
Before the end of the season?
A tender mist. Barely there
In the morning: a soft sun.

The husband I never think of
Returns one night in a dream
Who were those people? The moon above
The husband I never think of
Shines its indifferent love
Shines its unwavering beam.
The husband I never think of
Returns one night in a dream.

sun in the cedars
the moon in the pines
the day breaks itself clear
(sun in the cedars)
of the moon in the pines
and everyone sees again how it ends
the sun in the cedars
the moon in the pines

Have I been resting
My elbows in birdshit?
Are there birds nesting
Above, flinging direct hits
Where I have been resting
My arms? Was it a blue tit
What done it? I have been resting
My elbows in birdshit!

Was it merely personal
This interest in one's own life?
Each morning brought the same birdcall.
Was it merely personal
The persistent cardinal?
He sang in the cedars, a red knife.
Was it merely personal
This interest in one's own life?

The grandparents sink
Below the horizon
Like their parents before. Unlinked

To the earth, the grandparents sink,
What they were what we are soon indistinct.
The effort of living done
The grandparents sink
Below the horizon.

‧

Morning sun gone
Clouds in the hemlock
The wash undone
Morning sun gone
What should I have done—
Called the friend, taken a long walk?
Morning sun gone
Clouds in the hemlock.

‧

"Good looks will only get you so far
And that far I fully intend
To go." So she says, smoking in the car—
Good looks will only get you so far.
Scanning for lines in the mirror
She considers what Botox won't mend.
Good looks will get you only so far
Whatever you fully intend.

No escape from the endless chatter
Of people on cellphones
Talking as if it all mattered.
No escape from the chatter,
The world to be nattered
Away in a blizzard of blank tones.
No escape from the endless chatter
Of people. Cellphones.


Time to admit
That misanthropy
Has a logic to it.
Time to admit
Some days you'd quit
The species and flee.
Time to admit
That misanthropy.


What happens in one place
Will soon happen everywhere
Wrote the man with the seamed face.

What happens in one place
Will not be confined to that place,
Will spread and soon displace
What happens. One place
Will soon become everywhere.

—

Do you still think of me
As I still think of you
When I'm by the sea—
Do you still think of me
When you pass that stand of cherry trees
That bar on 81st only we knew—
Do you still think of me
As I still think of you?

—

Never again to visit that place
And never to think of it.
Never to see again that face
Never to visit that place
Never to try to stash the suitcase
In an overhead bin it won't fit.
Never again to visit that place
And never to think of it.

The language bore me along.
Before I knew anything
There was its welcoming song—
The language bore me along.
Strange to have gotten so wrong
So much, to know nothing
But language that bore me along
Before I knew anything.

Who were you to her
And who was she to me?
At 3 a.m. I wonder:
Who were you to her
And what did you murmur
To her when you suddenly saw me?
Who you were to her?
And who she was to me?

Those little crushes
That sneak up
Tiny ambushes

These little crushes
Betrayed by flushes
You can't cover up
Those little crushes
They sneak up

※

Five weathers in one afternoon—
A day seemed a year seemed a life
Seemed a cloud become a balloon—
Five weathers in one afternoon.
However it changes the moon
Rings its changes each riff less brief
Than the weather this afternoon.
A day seemed a year seemed a life.

※

Three and then four fell—
Dull thuds in the heat
That made the fruit swell.
Three and then four fell,
Loosed by the wind, the reddening apples
The deer come at dusk to eat.
Three and then four fell,
Sweet thuds in the heat.

Your tongue in my mouth
In the afternoon light
Your breath in my breath
Your tongue in my mouth
Your breast on my breast
In the unbreaking heat
Your tongue in my mouth
In the afternoon light

Not yet burnt red
The maple's tip, no frost
To flare it so. Not yet put to bed
The roses, not yet burnt red
The mountain, nor yet bled
Dry the pipes. No trees lost
This season's storms, nor yet burnt red
The maples tip. No frost.

And suddenly: Autumn,
The long endless sun over
And soon too the crickets' hum.

Thus suddenly: Autumn
Misgivings—so little begun
So little recovered
When suddenly: Autumn:
The long endless sun over.

# HAUNT

There are too many cedars here
hiding the sun hovering
over the dead
the lakes won't wash away
& the ghosts the locals talk of
are their memories
singing and shifting unbidden *I heard it*
last night *I saw it*
on the staircase
testimony weaving its own
shimmering cloth
we wear to keep ourselves warm
& to spare the others
our nakedness
—better not to have heard
the stories
the dead children
lunatic mothers gimlet-
eyed servants and
absentee lairds
the old murder ballads in Scotland
depend on
there's a dead soldier on auld fail dyke
on yonder greene plain

a knight centuries ago
there's a dead woman in the river
dead baby in the cradle
there's a dead soldier in the desert
& three crows wonder over and over
whether to cry out
an elegy
or to sit on his breastbone and pike out
his bonnie blue een

# SARATOGA AUGUST

rain rain and the trees
engulfed I am tired
of reading Russians their suffering
souls their tribulations
excavating a dank
depth they surely have a word for
that fatal Russian soul—
easy to see
how a blast of speed
called light might clear
the air the heavy hooves
of the horses now stopped
from racing a mile
away. Swaying
cedars, a light
wind and a low canopy
of clouds belie the summer
you recall from the calendar.
If I say spring
& you think September
you might be from Australia.
If I say love & you think sex
you are not Thomas Aquinas.
I am not worried

about my brain
today or TV or the latest war
in the Caucasus.
Creepy philosophers
isolatos in huts
articulate a theory
of care. I close
my eyes & the world
disappears.
You open yours
& the clouds rearrange
themselves shuffling
the birds.

wow the latest hysteria
our version of a rain dance
o it's coming friends the endless
rains we longed for danced for
& the deserts
we thought we knew
will be thickly forested
in the blink of some creature's eye—

geography's back
& new maps and the dolphin's
displaced by sick tones—

how anyone thought music
    meaningless
or universal    how anyone thought
    thought alone
would have everything to do with it—
    the wind picks up
    a cloudshift's sense
    transferring whatever—
    the helplessly metaphorical wind—


        ▪


that wind rushing through the trees
    was the rain. That sun you saw
through a cracked windowpane withdrew
    for days but only
from us. The specific ticks of raindrops
    individuating
themselves against the eaves ledges roof
    & beyond; behind
the indistinct fuzz of a general
    rain. What you call fog
he calls a cloud. What you call rain
    is raining every day


        ▪

rising up from below
the insistent swell of a downpour
now annihilating the flurry of pings
of a rain just seconds ago
distinguishable
from air

—

have I become a
        meteorologist
of moods no clear
        taxonomy or predictive
power to move out of
        this loafing groove

—

If I say rain
almost straight
for 14 days
you'll get a picture
not inaccurate though the sun's allowed
an almost daily swim
for a core crew
of lapswimmers.
Too bad for the divers

the funsters cannonballers
disciplined into invisible lanes
though Chana for one often veers
and merges without signaling—
Yo Chana! Watch out!
The yogi devised eight steps
to a clean heart and body
mere abstention from sex
insufficient. From the general drift
of talk it seems no one
is chaste or aspiring.
Fuckbuddies
there may be
but no one's really
prying; that's how we know
it's a reasonably genial
crowd—the gossip's
anthropological.

     Some nights poker,
other nights screenings, *Scenes*
*from a Marriage*, *George*
*Washington*, though some are dying
for a mindless buddy movie
some kickass comedy to purge
the blood burdened
with high thoughts.

     There's a fetus here

by which I mean a pregnant
dame—a gal I used to know
when I was 17 and cringing
at the dormroom door—
return of the repressed
indeedy. Little fetus
for now dubbed Oslo
by one and all
needn't screen out nada
right now unless he's freaked
by the talk in the Lino Room—
they say it like *rhino, lino*
for linoleum a residual
Britishism ghosting
this place that's lost
a lot of that crap. Today
I stumbled on the graves
of the founders, benefactors
—it must have been nice
to be here those years
not so nice with Robert Lowell
et al. on a manic
Commie-hunting spree.
No Russians here but in town
some waitresses have that Slavic
tilt to their eyes & in CVS
I encountered a blonde

so perfected it was clear
she was imported arm-candy
for one of the bigfellas
at the racetrack. Many here
are divorced
or will be & this is emotionally
difficult and statistical
like life
in general. No one touches
on this in the idyll unless
it won't break the spell
to invoke it. The cold
war's long over and meanwhile
it's just us chickens
brooding and happy
not to think
about what's next.


if I say thunder
and you answer lightning
were you already so near
I could touch you
—and *thunder*
& you turn off
your computer—

were you listening
to me or the weather
report? I'm not getting
any younger
says the thunder
to the sky—
I'm not moving
any farther says
the cloud that won't pass by


what god
takes these pictures
paparazzo
to the universe
violent bulbs
each bolt
flashing the black
world violet


among several games
a choice few
are favored—Poker, Mafia,
the occasional bout
of Boggle. Here

It's All Primates
All The Time
but the question
remains: bonobo
or chimp?
Have you hooked up
with S? M asked L
in the pool. Score one
for M! Soon
the inspectors
will arrive to measure
the chlorine, announce
all is well
or not. Meanwhile
the lapswimmers
swim on dreams
of Olympians spurring
their imperfect strokes
—utopian dreams
don't come from nowhere.
It turns out
the pool
inspector works in the local
liquor store—and here
he is, a beer
for all and tucked
in his pocket the chemical
testing strips.

Three down with rumored
Lyme but antibiotics are saving
us all from the worst
for the moment. If I say
we charmed the sun
with spells of guava rum
and grapefruit punch you should believe
it was a swell pool party last night
this morning's benediction of eggs
sunny side up
proving it so. If not everyone came
well that's OK, we can feel it
waning, the days, the months,
the season, our casually shared
lives. Intimations
of immortality are all very well
if all shall be well
but intimations of nothing
are more useful
if you have a residual
Calvinist soul. You don't need
to be a voluptuary
of death or dream or your dark
heart to want to know how its shaping
hand is shaping every hour. Heedless,

heedful, what's needful
is what we sometimes ask
when surfacing from a freestyle
lap, the pool bottoming
the abyss. O reason
not the need but can one help but reason
when it seizes the works and days
of our thinking. You'd never know
who was good in bed, at poker, at pool
unless you put yourself
through it. The sea calls
for drowning, the pool
for floating, some days
for lounging. If I say
cypress and you think
mourning you might read Latin.
If I say hemlock
and you think trees
and Socrates you will not be surprised
by our priceless ignorance.
Let us devote a week to nothing
that will not give pleasure.
Let us devote a life
to what's not to like
in this world if what's not to like in this world
is moving us into
the next—

and finally
sun
in the morning
proving
morning
after all
the time
of sunrises



see you've already forgotten
        the rain
in the cumulus courting
        the sun
it won't block—forgotten
        the pull
of the moon just past full
        is affecting
the waves. The song
        of the cardinal
flaring the hemlock so long
        ago rang out
so long ago nothing belongs
        to that rain

gone so long you've almost
forgotten
how long ago rained down
the rain

III

# DOUCE DAME

*Douce dame jolie,*
*Pour dieu ne pensés mie . . .*

GUILLAUME DE MACHAUT


Sweet love *douce dame*
      they used to say
before the canefields were flayed
      by slaves
whose songs made their way
      to all ears *douce dame*
in a court so elegant
      two ballplayers play
      for the king    for the gods
      & when one loses he falls
      —the rubber ball
      hard on the hip—
      & he dies so swiftly sacrificed
      the gods electrify themselves
      in waves of rage
*douce dame* I love you sadly
      love you long sweet love
old poets sang your name
      unattainable they're singing
      of elsewhere

the longing grown song
      in a room you won't come to
*douce dame* will I have you
    and what is having begetting
    a song in a wedding
no longer a song for this singing
how the whips raised the world the welts
    are still rising *douce dame jolie*
the music never stopped playing *douce dame*
    all century memory
sugared & honeyed for some *douce dame*
    by some measure
    *douce dame jolie*
    we've been here too long

# SPRING DAYBOOK

sun announcing
nothing but the sun announcing—
all is arrived

the tulips have opened their mouths
since the sun swept away the clouds
—divine prerogative asserted
in the allegory of a sky deserted
or if you wish full
of a pinkish
blue. hedged
by the boxwoods
the world is sufficient.
there is no deficiency
today's beam will not supply

green seine green
seine green the bronzes
in the park a bluer green the seine
than the yellow-green willow overhanging
the wall the island no longer insular

the bridges long ago built
can you smell the fires
singeing the clothes
of the Knights Templar
at the other end of the island
burnt alive


perhaps I too
am a shade

perhaps I am
too a shade


a species kind of day
        the humans
out and about in a quiver
        of solidarity
letting the arrows fly
        and fall where they may
they were styrofoam, unwounding
& we all went home whole
        after the game
        & those few beers that mark
        the end of a great & godforsaken day

■

all day the moon hung around
as if he too refused
to say goodbye
to such a perfect pasteled sky

window boxes overflowing
the iron trellises
tendrils echoing
the wrought scrolls

■

true they are thinner
than the usual run
of Americans walking
in the mall; and true
we usually stay in the inner
ring of the city balking
at going far out
of our quartier . . .
the takeout
is much better here . . .
one moves
into a perfect
comparative
mode

sun in the seine
in the seine a sudden scrap
of plastic sun the sun
reflecting the soda gone pop


yellow tulips scrambling
            to catch their fullblown
                        white brothers—
sibling allegory
            I impose on this garden
                        & now renounce

—lay your head on the flower bed
            my love
        the hyacinths are plying
                    the air & the bees
            are devoting their hours
                        to these newly sprung
                                    flowers

a small ripple of *francophonie*
lifts us out of the monotony
of the *policier*
& the *nouveau roman*
& flan after flan
turned out by a chef
grown complacent

&#9632;

we were having another conversation
about the conversations we weren't having

the laundry piled up, the dogs unwalked

&#9632;

sonic drift
a day's heft
not so difficult to lift
when not bereft

&#9632;

sky pinking out
        to a dusk
the blue day promised

forsythia spiking
      the air and the thin gilt swords
of the gods guarding and guiding
      the bridge into the twenty-first century—
        let us move to the light
    of an uncommon calendar
      roll back the hours
        the years
      unweep the tears


        ■


tulips slipped
their petals close
the cups shut
the pale yellow shell
of a day resolved


        ■


a gun tells the time—
shadow of a gun—
Palais Royal sundial

## PALAIS ROYAL

cooler april day and bright
clouddrift above the palace
reclaimed for all &
the bankers on lunch break
and grandmas with children
claim their public chairs
to bask in a strong sun—
a fountain dedicated to water
not the triumphs of kings
nor an allegory of continents
but water just this side
of the cultural making
the same rushing plash
the cascading rivers
of West Virginia
the Dry Fork and Laurel
made twenty years ago

# OTHER WORLDS

The edges
of other worlds
slicing the membranes
of my dreams
could I really release
their dimensions
if others have intentions
we are not aware of
no need
for an unconscious
with at least twelve universes
vibrating
along the seams
of the only one
I know I know

Heaven
a reasonable extrapolation
from the pulled
thoughts of theoretical
physicists
simply considered
another place
taking place

in the curved space
where parallels meet

Why not concede
if only here
the realists' defeat
"i am a strict realist
though not about everything"
sd the philosopher
there goes the world
independent
of my thoughts
that little space-
time given
a transcendental
a priori
only for rigorous
pietists ticking
away the last
minutes of the eighteenth century

Someone is rolling
dice someone
plays nicely
with friends
at the *école maternelle*
the kindergarten full

this year
of wanted children
europe more welcoming
of its daughters
than china or india
but let us not say
"they love them less"
what is the structure
love moves in
how long will the river
flow around
the rocks interests
pursued a need
to show the self
a singularity
amidst "the excess
of modernity"
language clotted
as the smashed caribbean
city stormbashed
*roulez les bon temps*
o my citizens
however we fashion
or abandon the day
we know not the time
but know the hour of our need

# JARDIN DU LUXEMBOURG

too early
bloomed
the cherry
halfsprung
soon
to be blasted
if predictions
of revivable
winter hold
the park
springstruck
the pollarded
planes the pond
aflutter
with ducks
there is no garden
like a formal garden
geometries
of desire
sharpened
to a point
you can't miss
your breath
escaped
remote
as clouds passing

# POUSSIN

clouds solid
as columns
the satyrs lounge
among     lunge
for the feel
of the seventeenth
century    tufts
of historical lust

# AU REVOIR

We did not go to Versailles.
The ocean did not turn over.
The moon remained unmanned
and two teams called out in turn Red Rover Red Rover.

Did Fisher-Price furnish our minds
with a transportable *imaginaire*?
George Bush the first said he liked pork rinds.
My name not Mary my self contrary.

Things are always terrible
for some people. The question
is the ratio of the palpable hurt
to the general session

of life in an era. Narcissism
the Hall of Mirrors multiplying
me and you and me no schism
between ourselves and our lying

ideals. This is another first-world poem
annoying in all its presumption
its feckless tourism presupposing a home
and its hubris misregarding itself as gumption.

Autobiography cannot anymore be spiritual
and the obviously sexual dimensions
of experience laid out before all
a spatchcocked chicken the cook mentioned

she'd make you for dinner
after she serviced the young monsieur
on the staircase. *It's hierarchy or chaos
mister* sd the structuralist seer

a woman no friend
to women but no enemy
either. How to end
the impasse. How to be

perfectly complicit to just the degree
you deserve asked the dominatrix
by which I mean post-structuralist
for whom the question of rubber vs. latex

moves us far beyond rational choice . . .

# WHAT A WONDER IS MAN (POEM ENDING

# WITH LINES FROM *ANTIGONE*)

so many nipples
one would never see
in London much less
Cleveland so many navels
ever fleshed in stone—

the stone breasts
of a thousand statues
succor the minds
of Parisian schoolchildren
impressions are everything
but the shape of what takes
cannot be known
in advance
the monoprint of the mind
reveals itself
a surprise even
to the expert eye
to the practiced hand
a print's a ghost
& stone is sand
is glass is gone

it may be the buildings
around us make us
or the mountain
air or the cheetos
compulsively eaten
what is a man
or woman beyond
an environment
distilled in a person?
a question
for the philosophers
open to something
that troubles
life. the blank
teenager who got
his gang to kill
a kid is it simply
las vegas at work
& the appalling mothers
"shopping 24/7
gambling 24/7
what's not to like?"
could he have loved
a woman like this
adam smith her lust
to traffic a perfect

example of sentimental
economic man—
*if things stand thus*
*what could I help*
*to do or undo*

# LIFE STUDY

Just as I must draw
to see
the world eclipse
itself before
my oblivious eyes
as I must draw to register
the retinal
flash of reality
effects my brain insists
on generating
to help me live
"life"
"not working out
too terribly well but I think
I'll keep going"
optimism
ridiculous
not to honor
the upsurge
as the dog frisks in the street
and the students smoke & glower & parse
their way
into situations
they forget

in a decade
but the smoke haze
lingering in the old walls of the rue Suger
however often cleaned
life
a revenge
upon memory
I disbelieve
in continuous
ribbons of identity
yet who else
did that past
happen to
waylay
last night
in the dream
that had me
up against the remembered wall

# JACARANDA

at the Place de la Contrescarpe
Jacaranda sign of your sexual misery
Jacaranda tree uninhabited by birds
Jacaranda the small pale purple bells descending the wind the
branch swaying
Jacaranda rhyming with that one tree I saw in a New England
cemetery
Jacaranda here you proliferate
Jacaranda your multiple purples
Jacaranda your little bells insisting on a spring ringing
Jacaranda whose name I heard on the lips of a sad wife
Jacaranda she did not know she was betrayed
Jacaranda but she knew the world rolled wrong
Jacaranda anchor us in the old true earth

The frizzle-sizzle
ménage: pansies and primulas
gone manic in the aisles
the gardeners monitor
by the Grand Hall
of Evolution—
          the names
tell the years
to the custodians
of our archives.
The book of flowers is closed
to those without eyes
for the colors displayed
above the raked dirt.
Root in the ground
though you will it gives nothing
you will not soon care to know.

Between Buffon
and Lamarck a rolling
lawn punctuated
with poppies drinking
the midday, the flagrant
oranges defying
an English rhyme

but not a French. Hybridize
the world let grafting
thrive. Invisible
genitals have plagued us
for centuries but is the remedy
the open show—

      let us conduct
our experiment second
by second on screens
that shimmer forth
the shaved vulvas.
A cabbage black
as a blackened brain
ill-preserved in the cabinet
of a cracked film
scientist: I saw a man
buy one at our local market.
I saw a man
acquire everything
he did not inherit.
I saw the flora gone
faunal springing
forth a monstrous
shrub. I saw us
grasping for names
at every garden's edge.

# FLÂNEUSE

The woman in the closely cut pink coat
            redeeming pink
for us all; a wish to have a drink
            at the café
deferred while a stroller ambles on
            passing a dog
who sniffs out his fellows' traces lacing
            the dank pavement—
invisible tracery but not unwhiffable.
            To leave a stink
a sociable sign of who passed here
            & recently
enough to be caught. Meanwhile the others eye
            the passersby
the skirts the scarves the perilous boots
            slipped and snapped
on the sensual thighs you can't touch
            without asking
if you too received the invitation
            the city
seems to be offering

# SAINT-SULPICE

in sun!
the coats thrown off the *fanfare* blasts its horns
& the organ with five manuals
   thunders or murmurs
   within as the maître decides
the eighteenth-century marvel still reigning
    o'er the tourists avid to see the replica
      of the Shroud of Turin &

Saint-Sulpice in sun!
   who would not rise on such a day
   to see the trees *défeuillés*

    but not for long with such
   a strong sun bathing the square the air
     the stickhockey boys in the warm honey
      of the almostsprung spring—

I thought of you Erika and Sébastien
   as I sat at the very café you mentioned
    *en face de* Saint-Sulpice
   so elegant your memories and your future—

the revolution—
    *vive la révolution!*
and the reconciliation of the old Catholics
    with the republicans
        perilously achieved and broken again
           and again
the Age of Revolutions brought to a close
    only by that war they used to call
        Great—

World War I!
Saint-Sulpice in sun!
    I tell you my love
        walking on the rue Suger
           this is a fine day
                to work and to play
        and St. Joseph is watching
        out for us all

           for the faithful
have left their petitions
    in the stone folds of his robes
        & on the somber marble
    they have inked their prayers
        no more war no more dying

graffiti for the 21st century
supplication
never out of fashion

between Yves Saint Laurent and my cracked brain
a new passion for strolling
in unimaginable clothes may be born

a very goddess from my brain!
And I would not reject a god

born of my thigh
nor one generated from a mitochondrial bit identical
to those of all my mothers
who survived their births
to see the sun
thus

Saint-Sulpice in sun!
where my mother has not been
but may yet come
where the *Annonciation* is happening forever
on video and *en ligne*
where the statues are pocked with bullet holes
but survive
as the sun still survives every shot we take at it

the sun imperishable
as the moon—the enviable sad moon! Saint-Sulpice by moon!
I hope to see you soon
you noble dead
     interred in rocky beds
     the decades make up
          as their own—

the stones above the bones below the sun above the sun below
the dizzy darkening in the blaze of the lordly moon
shining out of time out of merely human tune O give us a cadence
sweet maître of Saint-Sulpice
     in sun!

# RUE BONAPARTE

At the Place Sartre-
Beauvoir and the rue Bonaparte
I thought of you Celeste
at the Café Bonaparte!
The little dogs
seem less precious here
the smokers unabashed
the 15 shades of henna
one encounters every day
a riot of reds gone off—
A reassuring blinking
green cross: open
pharmacie; the red
illumination of the tabac—
O neon you are loving me
this hour! I have yet to see
a French person
in sneakers
unless I too easily assume
the unsneakered French . . .
I got Valéry
in my pocket
to see what the poets
of the 1920s are doing

these days . . .
Poem of the Mind . . .
Ah the great talkers . . .
The light is licking
the balustrades black
against the whitening
stones of the buildings
sustaining French history
so let's cross the street
and lay a grid of war
and toast the Napoleonic Code

# SONGS OF THE SOUTH

lavender freighted
with bees

pursuing their task
pursuing their pleasure
bee labor or leisure—
conundrum in the lavender
lavender conundrum

white butterflies
in the lavender

and now a derelict red
butterfly amidst the lavender bestarred
with white

and now amidst the lavender
bestarred with white butterflies
a derelict red butterfly

to what end
the white moths now alighting
in the lavender

II

no bees could labor
to make sweeter
the honey
your thighs


III

for white say wheat
for blue blé

I will mow your hay
my love
before the end of day


IV

poppies scattered
ungathered—

oleander
meander


V

Get Drunk the poet sd
and we did

IV

## PLOT (MOUNT AUBURN CEMETERY)

the sleep of the just
    and the lost at sea
    and the mediocre dead
undisturbed by mexican gardeners
    who will never be buried here
    nor in michoacán

the weeping beech
    weeps not for thee
    nor me nor any tree
but weeps an english eye
    a name stuck in the throat
earthclot lifeblot inkspot

# CONTACT

and sex once
a day a week a
month a year
goes by and one
hyacinth only
returns, frail
blue against the militant
grass that does cover all
in the residential
precinct of the
New England town
its roads long paved
old Indian trails the steps
they took toward
us the first
exchange for a fish
two biscuits

# TRANSCENDENTALISM

I have seen something brighter
than realism
would allow

another train another
sunset pulling the world
to its edge renewable
as the faithful
pledge faith in the
dawn they hope to see—

prismatic seeping
away to a gray-
scale backlit
a pinkish tinge
giving the day's
game away—

pioneer birch
congregation
by the tracks
hardy thin
New England
sentinels salute
those passing thru

too late too late
the redwing blackbird
burred
in the reeds ringing
the reservoir

organizing the air
around the golfers
a duet of geese
pausing as they flew over
one descending chromatic legato
the other's staccato blats
winged horns
making even the Sunday golfers
suspend their swing

| Snow | Geese | Pines |
| Geese | Snow | Pines |
| Pines | Snow | Geese |
| Snow | Pines | Geese |
| Geese | Pines | Snow |
| Pines | Geese | Snow |

within I heard
the geese outside
emigrants or
remigrants who's
native in this clime
better to say
seasonal singer passing
through what's passing—

that other life
I did not live
its shadow grows
as long as life

& unlike hindus
what I've done
will not translate
beyond this place
nor will survive
this once this time

to each her heaven
mistake to think
salvation singular
heaven hybridizes
the creatures composite
aggregates of all
answering pains
and hands extended
remade bodies
identity undissolved
solved and revealed
as the surfeit

nomadic
subjectivity
a liberty
ungiven me
unreleased
to a century
of new forms
for the free

# AFTER SEAN SCULLY:

## "YOU HAVE HAD YOUR DAY . . ."

a bar
on 3rd
a beer
or two
first down
and ten
number
the number
of Sundays
unchurched
uneven
unmarked
"each day
a short life"

## SO LONG

these intricate flowers
shining in the shadowed hours
of another day, fatal excess
of the lucky in the west

with gardens and welfare
not yet collapsed . . . fare
thee well old thoughts
and be with us still

in the web the porn-king
spun    What girl pricking
her finger on a spinning wheel
would not sell her twat or model?

*everything you want I want*
is the headline the cunt
of the world obscene
in old meters the screen

unblank & minds buzzing.
a whiplashing wind blows
through the brain festering
with botched thought westering

like the intangible sun—
old sun we have not begun
to hurt you yet. the moon
flagspiked tells another story

salutes the latest platoon
from the orbited. Blasted
into space let's see the moon
with our own face observe the last

man exiting the human race . . .

# IT'S NOT THAT

It's not that I'm opposed
to poison in my lips

or pig in my soap—
it's not that I'm opposed.

It's not that I'm opposed
to plastic bottles that won't decompose

to malodorous phosphorus flows—
it's not that I'm opposed

to what you propose—
surgery on your imperfect nose

favelas blasted
with hoses—it's not that

I'm opposed to opposing
the opposite of anonymous

neighbors, the nosy stargazers
who discover new celebrity planets

about to crash into your car. It's not that
I'm opposed that we drive

when it's not very far
to walk or bike not opposed

you're opposed to the subway
the stink of the general—

train 4, 5, or 6—not opposed
to the sex on Craigslist

to your pets' special tricks
to the organized slaughter of cows

by the tenderest machines—
not opposed to your dreams

to their screams to our hopes
not opposed to the hordes

with their ropes knives and bombs
set in desolate streets slums

and thrumming towns not opposed
to your proms and baptisms

to ongoing Christian schisms
most unopposed to fierce Muslims

Jews Baha'is and Hindus posed
in poses temples now oppose

the Kama Sutra too ooh-la-la
for the petit-bourgeois members of the BJP

—not opposed to a big GDP
to a loud ATV not opposed to anything

I can see hear or touch
to "enough or too much"—

It's not that I'm opposed
to whatever I should propose

opposing, knowing
knowing is thinning

in the species' extra inning
on a world slow spinning on an

axis slightly tilting
into folly so is it folly

to suppose you could oppose
proposing something to oppose

# ANTHROPOLOGY

why am I not preserving
    the yanomami language
    or speakers of same
or learning a lusty romance tongue
    the smell of the sea
    mediterraneanizing open vocables
        split down the middle
        by dirt?
o the language game uh huh. I played
    the lion, saw that I won, sd
    hello. He like unto himself
        yawned/roared
        as the case required.
a daggered paw ripped off my face
    the savanna no longer so peaceful—


all this was caught by the cameras
    the intrepid documentarian brought
    in the jeep.


bleep bleep went the machine
    begging for love
    thought the anthropomorphizers.

and right they were: desire slimed
everything.
how stupid to forget the objects
would one day rise up

# PILGRIMAGE

the local stone all mined
they found another quarry
for repairing the abbey
the river winds behind
the unchristianed welsh long dead
and the burgundian monks too
though the river keeps its course
more or less
and through the masonry
that once sustained
a clerestory
the sun shines
unimpeded by glass
or a human past
and those wisps
you might have
thought clouds
reveal themselves
the fading smoke
of a jet just beyond
our view

■

to see the place
disappointed
nothing

■

where the monks cooked
a plaque—
an image
from an illuminated ms—
a fox quartered—
grinning—
how they did it

■

beyond Tintern
the Severn

beyond the Wye
historical sky

■

flax field
a roman shield
celtic goddess
stoploss

white horse
on the hill—
paleo-,
neo-?

V

.

.

.

# MEDITATION/CENTRAL PARK

The willows clipped
unyellowed peculiar
their hair so blunt
above the zamboni'd
ice. The orange flame
of the maples the poets
restored to their walk
amidst the endangered
American elms—
Central Park almost
the perpetual habitus
of the milling citizenry.
No skating now but staring
at the slaked ice smoothed
for practice and tricks.
The strongminded men
who considered
the republic something
to cherish still live
and the women beside.

And now they fly out
the first skaters accomplished
gliders the tracks they make

in the moment delible,
delicate. Nostalgia
to think it was otherwise
or true. The state
loves its people
whether the people
know. The state forsakes
the people not its people
and they know it in the gardens
of L.A. and they know it
in the kitchens of NY
the toilets the treelimbs
and truckstops and orchards
the mountains
of pears unharvested
because laborers this year
did not come. Strange
to live in historical skin
the freckles the age spots
the pale privilege made
by ancestors I cannot name.

And now the boys bent
over clubbed sticks slide
back and forth imaginary
pucks pushing. Keep
to the path Do not endanger

the elms of North America
Do not speak loosely
of your neighbor's stupidity
Do not forget to vote
with your feet and cash
in hand. The labor
theory of value reveals
itself an artifact
of 19th C. thought perfected
like the nation-state
like the realist novel
some of us still live in.

# FUCKWIND

in the teen comedy
pregnancy was a metaphor
for an obstacle
& a beginning and the tears
escaped despite
our lifelong
defenses. As if
there'd be no scar . . .
As if romance
would begin again
& again & the world
retain its blooming
cherries and succeeding
dogwoods the youth
of the day
unrevenged. Envy
is too little pondered
as a human
engine and the future
too open is lashed
shut by a shuddering
wind we take
as punishing
when it's only the indifferent

wind. Imaginary natives
attending the world
we call local
know every taste
and ripple of each wind
we simply call wind.
In my next life
I will come
with big eyes & wide ears
and nothing will escape
my attention & all the names
will flower on my fluent
tongue, fuckwind.
Today I'll say
wind is the wind
that winds through
every sharp breath
I'm taken by

## MOONRISE LAKE CHAMPLAIN

The moon will rise soon
in the southeast. A day
done in common
measure. The wild chicory
blueing the roadside the
sky now blue will pink
into a dark sea for the moon
to rise in. The titanium
white triangles of starched
sails silently parse
the lake, the north wind
lulled. Few salmon this year
and none legal for eating
& all bristling with
lampreys. The composition's
wrong the old balance
off the new mussels
eating the lake clear
of the algae we need
the specialist says
on the radio.
I would not have known
what we need
but for your reports

and my guesses. These
are often wrong including
predictions for tomorrow
the windspeed and rain.
The lights are shining
from the neighboring
state the green mountains gone
into a range of ever less green
blues pasted in a
suddenly Japanese sky.

# LUNAR MARIA

*—large, dark, basaltic plains on Earth's Moon, formed by ancient volcanic eruptions. They were dubbed* mária, *Latin for "seas," by early astronomers who mistook them for actual seas.* ADAPTED FROM WIKIPEDIA

Rose red the moon
rose low in the east
rose a finale all in blue
but cool self-contained
as the moon immemorial
red the moon and dark blue
the craters they call *mária*
imagining seas to float
moonmen Rose red and pasted
the sky like a peaceable
wafer, red heading to
orange away from our blood
pulsing and shed. Over the harbor
the mountains & into
the unstarred black see it
mounting & rising describing
the night with the one face
it's thus far shown men.

Red the unbombed moon
& red the trick the sun's
played on basalt
the mineral realities gone
orange an alien eye
the wolf shows you
in the forest—Red
in August the moon
unimpeded Red the measured
moon its late debut none too soon
for the waning month
Red the remote rock
we cling to thus far
permanent as the sun

# LATE OCTOBER

The blues are sifting
the night mountain
and lake and my cold hands
will not be warm soon.
The tender cats
will go to new caretakers
I do not know
and in another life
punishment awaits
this and other plans.
I do not know
what I think
is what I thought in the car
your turns of phrase forcing
my mind away from a too
quickly slid into
groove. By the sheltered
great camp the robber
baron carved out of the
wilderness the trail
by the lake a pillow
of pine needles gone tawn—
I have laid my head
in such a bed

by a city reservoir
an unfenced pond
a century before
and I have seen you
in that city but not where you are
saying you are. Unleafed
the maples or stripped
depending on wind
and the angle
you feel. I do not know
what I feel but I feel
until I don't then relief
the body merely body
unbidden and bent
to some task worth
thanksgiving.


From here I see the tone
I adopted was the air
I was breathing
unknowing half knowing
the intervals thinning
the careful gradations
lost. I am not talking
about glissandos
or low-down

slides but the paring
away of the colors
all of us once knew
on a transcendental palette
yet to be imagined.
A soft rain
in a cold air audible
in the dusk the squirrels
thumping the roof attesting
it's time to lay stores.
The fire on the mountain
dimming and the season
hunting its way to the
monochrome winter
slowly reveals a glitter
of gray scales gone blue
in unbearable noon.
I have stood there
on skis on a groomed trail grateful
for boys in their robust machines
tending to our pleasure
and taking their own
in the logging camp reclaimed
for leisure. I wonder if I am living
a life or living
and what kind of question
or quest becomes a person

who seeks but can't make
a clear thing. Cold
in the earlier dark
a braced thought holds
itself in a chair built
around the thought
of a body awaited there.

# PASSAGE III

cold birds
still sing

a bright sun
chill air

snow entombing
precocious crocuses

tricked
by a spring

now
falsened


cherry trees . . .
Good Friday . . .
—treatise: on the use of trees

a flyblown carcass
in the underbrush below
the cypress in the cemetery
: the dead above
: the dead below

          ■

like a Fantin-Latour
the clutch of flowers
in your hand
and apple frothing the air

          ■

the life you're not leading
the blood you're not bleeding
the knot you're not kneading
the mouth you're not feeding
the earth you're not seeding

          ■

they're grooming the lawns
     for the graduates
          and the proud parents
and meanwhile the yellowthroat sings
      unconcerned—

cherries just gone by their faded blossoms
thick against the
insurgent leaves
offer the very figure
of spring melancholy
o I missed
when they were fully in bloom
& the season
& the time for the
perfect spring
haiku
to hail another winter
survived

where among the redbud blooms exploding
along the thin branches
is my death written

earth conspiring
against me
have a child
to load
the earth
with vines
with lives
with signs songs & cries

insistent crow

cardinal whoop

peepers booming open the night

 stabbing life into your heart

 the odious air

 reverberant



that was no song

but an alarm call



the rhythmic thunk of the basketball

 thwacking the tarmac

 at the little park a

  block over

 ... boys ... calls ...

and the rain holding off—

 a May nor'easter

deferring the fullest spring

 we might have had but leaving

  the lilacs to extend

  their delicate

                    thrusting
                into the air
            the boys birds and blossoms share


                        ▪


say that a heron perched
            immobile
            until
            alert the head
            turns


                        ▪


the weather is far more violent
here and present
or so it seems days
one's attention is open
to the cloudthrottled air
lit by a near-equinoctial
sun—the nights
too extend to a farther
horizon the stars legible
in this particular sky
to those able and wishing
to scry. too many years
looking inward thinning

the lexicon of the visible
world its oracular
reality sounding
itself all along

these maples
that stone
that garden fountain
the mists rolling in
over the mountains
disguising the sky
the world
gone slate
its greens drained
as that fountain
before the first frost
the rain is passing
and the lilacs
the thunder
the day but what
have you held
beheld beset
as you are
by yourself

signing
*my best*
*beset*
instead
reveals
itself the key
an extra *e*
lone vowel
tiny howl
I did not do
what my hands did

         ▪

wavelap and lakeslap lick
     the ear; the air carries
         stripes in the
       low precincts of sky—
a mower blares somewhere
     above A and
        shuts off a
   shock of
       silence
into which the wave-
     slaps surge

         ▪

*to enter the water*
in Mayan
*to die*

■

over there the gray
        gathering
                sheath meant
                        rain
but our private sun
        continues to sign-
post a clear day at least
        for us.
an earthquake
        in China
                means
        precisely what
                to me
        wondered Adam Smith—
the world disappearing
        the instant my tooth aches: Sartre

my skin some days
                extends
        as wide as the sea
and the waves of the world

roll through, equable
terrible
but I am living this narrow
life and no other
except yours I imagine
some days we're graced
or grazed by a shared bullet


■


today no thrush silvered the air
in the woods
the wind blowing hard
against the bike
passing a stretch of field
where tractors for miles around
come to die
the iron congregation rusting
faithful as the grass.
the cows at Saywards Farm seemed
too confined
why aren't they grazing in the field and why
are their calves
wired in—
late last night
after the sunset
I did not see

the lake took on that babyish blue
         I so love and I saw
a sole balloon aloft lifting over Vergennes
         puffing by Camel's Hump
and heading east—
               we have harnessed the air
                       for our pleasure
                       our leisure a rhyme
               with the weather
                       clearing as if the
                       skies cared
                       or could


                       ▪


radios and weathervanes
conduct the air
disperse *manes*


                       ▪


mountains deforested
         by distance
Hokusai shapes cut
         against the
         sky the clouds
                 address just
         so

and through the same air
      the radio pours
      its usual brew of cheer & death
      what wonder little schizo
        you reel so
      in the fractured world
the sky bends to my way
      and to yours and to home
      sweet home

my soul marching through
the open fifths of its salvation
shapenotes shaping
me home

not the sun but the sun
      in the river
not the moon
      but the lake-swallowed moon
the stars cracking open the black paved road
      where immortals strode

# ENVOI

the vanish
of the shore-

drift the last
rift unsutured

assured the cloud

knowing goes in
song in stars inscaped

---

clouds gathering
do I go
with the gathering
clouds or the sun
seen an hour
ago

# NOTES

28 In "Songs of a Season II," "Do you still think of me / As I still think of you"; see Elizabeth Barrett Browning, "L.E.L.'s Last Question."

33–34 "Haunt": see Child Ballad No. 26, "The Three Ravens" / "The Twa Corbies."

51 "Douce Dame": "in a court so elegant . . ." invokes an ancient Meso-american ballgame, a variety of which was played by the Aztecs.

93 "After Sean Scully": after Scully's remarks included in his Wall of Light exhibition at the Metropolitan Museum of Art, 2006–2007.

110–11 "Fuckwind": an old Northern English word for a small falcon or kestrel; or also, perhaps, a species of wind. Thanks to Tom Pickard.

# ACKNOWLEDGMENTS

I am grateful to the editors of the following journals, i
these poems first appeared, sometimes in slightly diff
*American Scholar*, *jubilat*, *The New Yorker*, and *A Publi*
du Luxembourg" appeared in *A Sheaf for Melissa* (Ar
2007).

I would like to thank the Yaddo Corporation; the Mac
and the Columbia Institute for Scholars at Reid Hall, Pari
erosity and support: parts of this book were written duri
cies they sponsored. My gratitude as well to Jeff Clark (ag
Compagnon; and to Chana Bloch, Adam Davies, Lan
Cathy Park Hong, and Erica Mena. And best thanks to Jor
who shows how "*ai presenti diletti / la breve età commett[e*

And first and last, *per sempre, per l'aura non amara m*